SCHOOL CAMP

REINALDO DOMINGOS

ILLUSTRATION: PATRICIA PESSOA

Author | Reinaldo Domingos

Pedagogical director | Ana Rosa Vilches

Editorial coordinator | Renata de Sá

Translator | Jamie Lee Searle

Art editor | Beatrice Jacob

Editor | Renata de Sá

Proofreading | Shalimar Fodrá

INTERNATIONAL CATALOGING DATA IN THE PUBLICATION (CIP)
(CÂMARA BRASILEIRA DO LIVRO, SP, BRAZIL)

Domingos, Reinaldo
School camp / Reinaldo Domingos ; Illustration: Patrícia Pessoa; Translation: Jamie Lee Searle. --São Paulo: Editora DSOP, 2019.
Original Title: O colecionador de sonhos.
ISBN 978-85-8276-340-7

1. Money - Children's literature
2. Finances - Children's literature
I. Pessoa, Patricia. II. Searle, Jamie Lee. III. Title.

19-30368 CDD-028.5

CONTENTS FOR SYSTEMATIC CATALOGUE

1. Money - Children's literaturel 028.5
2. Finances - Children's literature 028.5

Iolanda Rodrigues Biode - Librarian - CRB-8/10014

DEAR READER

MY NAME IS REINALDO, AND JUST LIKE YOU, I WAS ONCE A CHILD. FROM A YOUNG AGE, I LIKED TO INVENT STORIES AND CREATE IMAGINARY WORLDS. AS I GREW UP, ONE OF MY GREATEST DREAMS WAS TO SHARE THESE STORIES WITH ALL CHILDREN.

I MADE THIS DREAM COME TRUE. YOU TOO HAVE THE ABILITY TO ACCOMPLISH ALL YOUR DREAMS AND MAKE THEM A REALITY. ALL YOU NEED TO DO IS FOLLOW THE FOUR STEPS I CREATED, WHICH YOU WILL FIND INSIDE THIS BOOK.

AS WELL AS HELPING YOU TO ACCOMPLISH YOUR DREAMS, I WOULD ALSO LIKE TO INVITE YOU TO TAKE PART IN THIS STORY WITH ME – BY PAINTING AND DRAWING...

I HOPE YOU ENJOY IT.

ALL THE VERY BEST,
REINALDO DOMINGOS

NICO WAKES UP EARLY FOR HIS FIRST DAY AT SCHOOL.

THE SCHOOL IS FUN AND NICO IS HAPPY WITH HIS NEW FRIENDS: ISA, MATT AND MONICA.

A i O U
1 3 4 5 6 7 8 9 0
D S O P

NICO THINKS:

WOW, MY SISTER'S DREAM IS GREAT. SPENDING A DAY IN THE COUNTRYSIDE WITH HER CLASSMATES.

BUT NICO AND HIS FRIENDS CAN'T GO, BECAUSE THEY'RE TOO YOUNG.

THEY HAVE A GREAT IDEA, AND
NICO DECIDES TO SHARE IT
WITH HIS GRANDPA.

NICO:

– WE HAVE 30 DAYS FOR THE SCHOOL CAMP IN THE SPORTS HALL.

AH WAIT... I DON'T HAVE A SLEEPING BAG FOR CAMP NIGHT.

GRANDPA:

– YOU KNOW WHAT YOU NEED TO DO, GRANDSON...

NICO:

– OH YES. I CAN USE THE DSOP 4 STEPS TO MAKE MY DREAMS COME TRUE.

1. DIAGNOSE – I DON'T HAVE A SLEEPING BAG.
2. DREAM – A SLEEPING BAG.
3. BUDGET – THERE ARE 30 DAYS LEFT TO GET A SLEEPING BAG.

– DO NOT FORGET SAVE, HERE ARE SOME COINS FOR YOUR FROG BANK – SAYS GRANDPA.

SLEEPING
BAG

RECYCLE
HERE

NICO'S MOTHER TELLS THE KIDS
ABOUT THE RECYCLING MACHINE.

THE BIG NIGHT ARRIVES.

NICO, HIS FRIENDS AND THEIR TEACHER ARE HAVING FUN.

THEY PLAY CIRCLE GAMES, TELL STORIES, HAVE A PICNIC...

– NICO, WHY ARE YOU AWAKE? – ASKS ISA.

– I CAN'T SLEEP – SAYS NICO.

– LET'S COUNT SHEEP – SAYS MONICA.

– GOOD IDEA – SAY HIS FRIENDS.

NICO DISCOVERS THE VALUE OF FRIENDSHIP.

REINALDO DOMINGOS

REINALDO DOMINGOS WAS BORN IN CASA BRANCA, A CITY IN THE STATE OF SÃO PAULO, BRAZIL. HIS FATHER WAS A RAILWAY WORKER AND HIS MOTHER WAS SELF-EMPLOYED. AT THE AGE OF 12, HE DREAMED OF HAVING A BIKE. HE ADOPTED THE STRATEGY OF SAVING SOME OF HIS MONEY EVERY MONTH TO ACCOMPLISH HIS DREAM. THIS BECAME THE BASIS OF THE DSOP METHODOLOGY: A SIMPLE AND EFFICIENT WAY OF MANAGING MONEY, CHANGING CONSUMPTION HABITS AND MAKING DREAMS COME TRUE.

ACTIVITIES

1. WHAT DOES NICO NEED AT SCHOOL? DRAW A GREEN CIRCLE AROUND IT.

2. HELP NICO TO GET DRESSED.

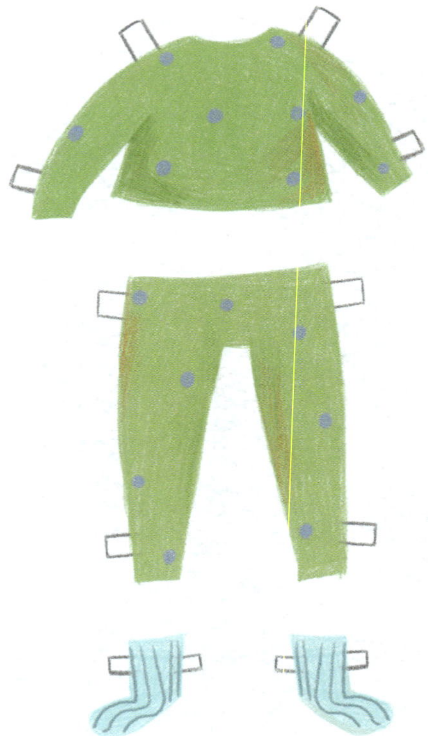

3. DRAW NICO'S PATH.

4. DRAW A BLUE SQUARE AROUND NICO'S DREAM.

5. COLOUR THE MONEY BOXES: A GREEN FROG, A YELLOW CHICK AND A BLUE WHALE.

A VERY SPECIAL MESSAGE FROM DSOP

To the teachers or parents or guardians

Congratulations, you just took the first step towards an investment with an invaluable return: prosperity, in every moment of your family's life, beginning with your young student!

The DSOP methodology illustrates how important it is to have dreams in our lives, and above all how to achieve them. It focuses upon behavioural development, with the goal of creating a healthier financial life. This makes it possible to build a life filled with accomplishments.

The DSOP books, courses and educational programmes for children and young people also include content which extends to family members and school staff. The guidance given, both in the manuals and projects offered to teachers and from the DSOP advisors and pedagogical support team, will help your young student to transform their life, inspired by the captivating and entrepreneurial paths taken by the characters in the stories.

There is growing awareness internationally of the importance of incorporating Financial Education in school curriculums. In some cases, this

MENSAGEM MUITO ESPECIAL DA DSOP

Aos responsáveis pelos alunos ou seus familiares

Parabéns, você acaba de dar o primeiro passo rumo a um investimento de retorno inestimável: a prosperidade em todos os momentos da vida da sua família, começando pelo jovem estudante da sua casa!

A metodologia DSOP mostra a importância dos sonhos em nossas vidas e, especialmente, como alcançá-los. O foco está no desenvolvimento comportamental para uma vida financeira mais saudável. Assim, é possível construir uma vida cheia de realizações.

Os livros, cursos e programas educacionais para crianças e jovens também são complementados por conteúdos que se estendem à suas famílias e funcionários da escola. Com o apoio das orientações dos manuais e projetos oferecidos aos professores e da assessoria e suporte pedagógicos da DSOP, eles ajudarão seu jovem estudante a transformar sua vida inspirado nas adoráveis trajetórias empreendedoras das personagens.

A BNCC (Base Nacional Comum Curricular) tornou obrigatório nas escolas públicas e privadas o ensino de Educação Financeira nos Anos Iniciais e Finais do Ensino Fundamental, porém voltada a que os alunos desenvolvam comportamento de consumo consciente. A própria ONU propõe os 17

MENSAJE MUY ESPECIAL DE DSOP

A las familias de los alumnos o sus responsables

Felicitaciones! Usted acaba de dar el primer paso rumbo a una inversión de valor inestimable: la prosperidad en todos los momentos de la vida de su familia, empezando por los jóvenes estudiantes de su casa.

La metodología DSOP potencia la valoración de los sueños en nuestras vidas y, especialmente, cómo alcanzarlos. El énfasis está en el desarrollo comportamental hacia una vida financiera más saludable, pues así es posible construir una vida de realizaciones. Los libros, cursos y programas educacionales para jóvenes son también complementados por contenidos que alcanzan a sus familias y toda la comunidad escolar.

Con el apoyo de las orientaciones de los manuales, proyectos, asesoría y soporte pedagógicos de la Editorial DSOP, los profesores ayudarán a su joven estudiante a transformar su vida, inspirado en las adorables trayectorias emprendedoras de los personajes.

En Brasil hay leyes que han vuelto obligatoria en las escuelas públicas y privadas la enseñanza de la Educación Financiera volcada hacia el desarrollo de un comportamiento de consumo consciente.

is combined with teaching students to develop conscious behaviour around consumption practices. The UN proposed the 17 Sustainable Development Goals (SNGs) and included Responsible Consumption, referring to precisely this objective.

For over 10 years, Reinaldo Domingos PhD has been sharing his methodology with the world via the DSOP group. It has brought great success not only for him, but also for all the Financial Educators and Financial Therapists who have graduated during this decade, as well as, more recently, through franchises. Its efficiency has been proven not only in practice, but also by the academic and scientific world; his methodology has been championed in the United States at universally commended master, doctoral and post-doctoral levels.

When it comes to behaviour, the best way to develop it swiftly and achieve efficient results is to start as early as possible and maintain consistency. We need to begin preparing ourselves for adult life in childhood, and by doing so we can achieve financial independence earlier than previous generations, and dedicate our efforts and time towards realising our own dreams and those of the people we love.

So, how does this transformational methodology work?

Learn more and win a free e-book on DSOP Financial Education Methodology, visit the link or QR Code on the back cover of this book.

Objetivos de Sustentabilidade para a Humanidade e incluiu o Consumption, referindo-se exatamente a esse objetivo.

Há mais de 10 anos, por meio do Grupo DSOP, o *PHD* Reinaldo Domingos tem compartilhado com o mundo sua metodologia vivenciada com sucesso não só por ele, como também por todos os Educadores Financeiros e Terapeutas Financeiros formados ao longo dessa década, além do trabalho mais recente com os franqueados. Não só a prática comprovou sua eficiência, mas também o mundo acadêmico e científico, pois sua metodologia também foi defendida nos Estados Unidos em níveis de mestrado, doutorado e pós doutorado aprovados com louvor e de forma unânime.

Quando falamos de comportamento, a melhor maneira de desenvolvê-lo mais rapidamente rumo a resultados eficientes é começando o quanto antes e mantendo a continuidade. Desde crianças temos que nos preparar para a vida adulta, assim, poderemos nos tornar independentes mais cedo que as gerações anteriores e direcionaremos nossos esforços e tempo a partir de então para a realização de sonhos próprios e das pessoas que amamos.

Mas, como é essa metodologia transformadora?

Saiba mais e ganhe um e-book sobre a Metodologia DSOP de Educação Financeira por meio do QR Code atrás deste livro.

La misma ONU propone 17 Objetivos de Sustentabilidad para la Humanidad e incluye *Consumption*, refiriéndose exactamente a esa cuestión.

Hace más de 10 años, por medio del Grupo DSOP, el PHD Reinaldo Domingos ha compartido su metodología vivenciada con éxito no solo por él sino por todos los Educadores Financieros y Terapeutas financieros formados en sus cursos. Además de toda la comprobación práctica, está también el reconocimiento académico y científico, pues la Metodología DSOP ha sido defendida en los EEUU en niveles de máster, de doctorado y posdoctorado.

Cuando se trata de comportamiento, para garantizar resultados eficientes en el futuro, lo mejor es desarrollarlo lo más pronto posible, además de mantener su continuidad. Desde niños, debemos ir preparándonos para los principales retos de la vida adulta, para volvernos independientes financieramente aún antes de la edad en la que las generaciones anteriores lo lograban. Así, podremos concentrarnos a partir de entonces no solo en disfrutar de los sueños ya alcanzados, sino también a multiplicarlos e incluir a quienes amamos en esa trayectoria.

Pero, cómo es esa metodología transformadora? Para saberlo, infórmese mejor y adquiera su e-book sobre Educación Financiera en el código QR detrás de este libro.

EVERY CHILD HAS THE RIGHT

TO DREAM, AND TO MAKE THOSE DREAMS COME TRUE